NUMBERS 1-10

HAPPY READING FOR AGE 2- 5

KRITHI DHEERAJ

ISBN 979-888546031-6

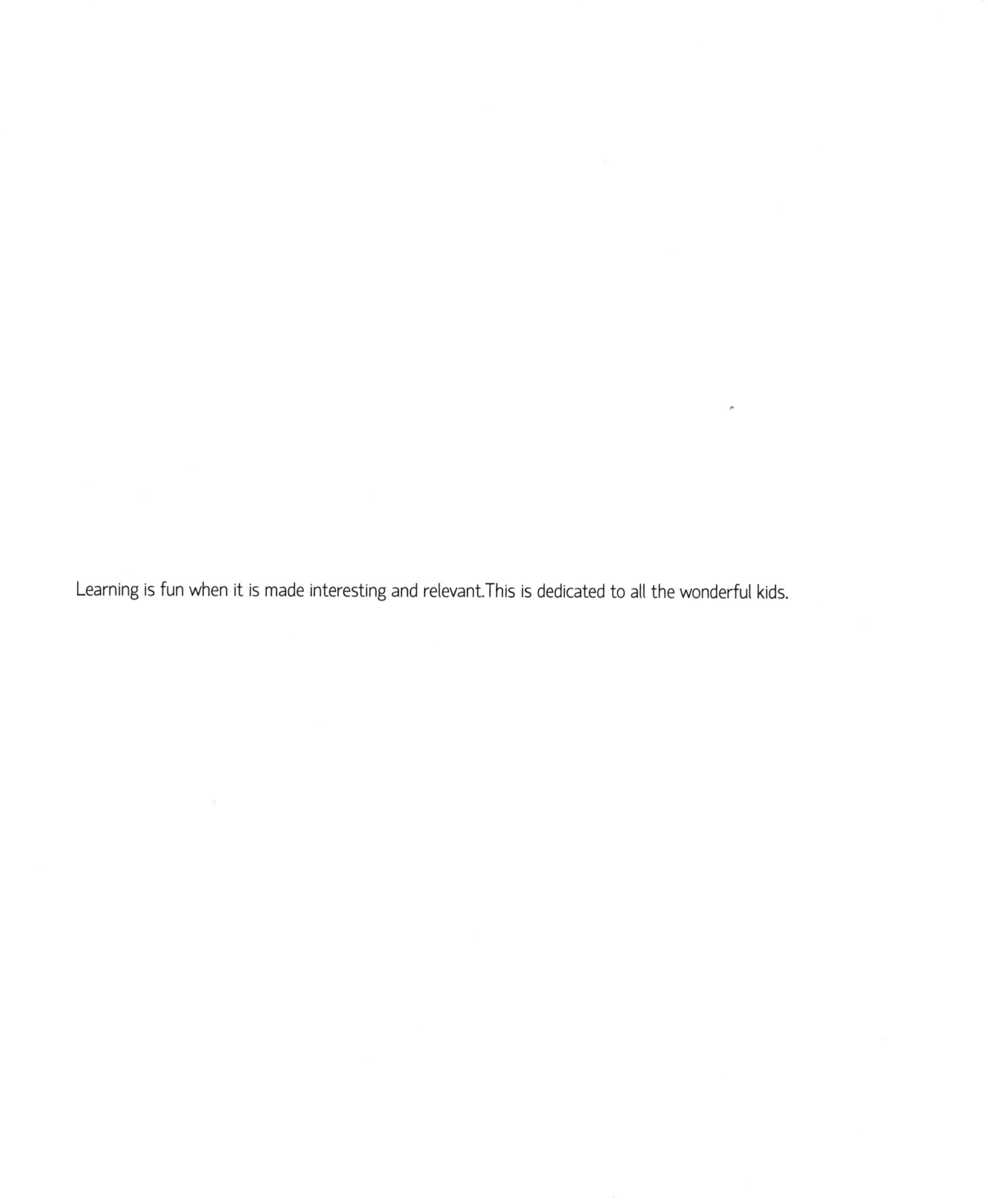

Learning is fun when it is made interesting and relevant.This is dedicated to all the wonderful kids.

Contents

Acknowledgements

I have always believed books are our best friends. It is even better when it is introduced to kids at very young age .My own kid has been very fond of books when he was a toddler. This has inspired me to bring out this book hoping that it will instigate learning habit in kids which will be fun and interesting.

CHAPTER ONE

Number One

Once upon a time , there was a park in which there was a tree which was very lonely . It was very sad that there was no one who would come near it . The tree had green leaves and gave nice shade.

One tree

CHAPTER TWO

Number Two

Let's see who had come to this park early in the morning.Wow! there came two parrots . Looked like both the parrots were friends and they had come to the park in search of some green tree to rest.

Two parrots

CHAPTER THREE

Number Three

The parrots were happily enjoying the fresh air and lush green leaves of the tree . The parrots suddenly saw some cars entering near the park. They were eager to see who was it . There came threee red cars.

Three red cars

CHAPTER FOUR

Number Four

The two parrots peeped to see who was there in the car. They could see four boys happily getting out of the cars.Looked like they were very eager to play in the park.

Four boys

CHAPTER FIVE

Number Five

The boys carried five colourful balls with them. They came near the tree on which the two parrots were sitting .The boys started playing under the tree.The tree was very happy to see the kids.The kids saw the parrots and said ,"Hey ! look at the parrots .They look so adorable".

Five balls

CHAPTER SIX

Number Six

Oh no! it started raining .The kids took shelter under the tree .They had four umbrellas with them .They opened the umbrellas . They saw two more people sitting on the park's bench also opening their two umbrellas. It was a colourful sight to see six umbrellas rising high up in the sky splashing rain water.

Six umbrellas

CHAPTER SEVEN

Number Seven

The boys were waiting for the rain to stop . However, they were hungry by then.One of the kid opened his bag .He was happy to see that he had seven apples.He gave one each to all his friends .They enjoyed the delicious juicy red apples.

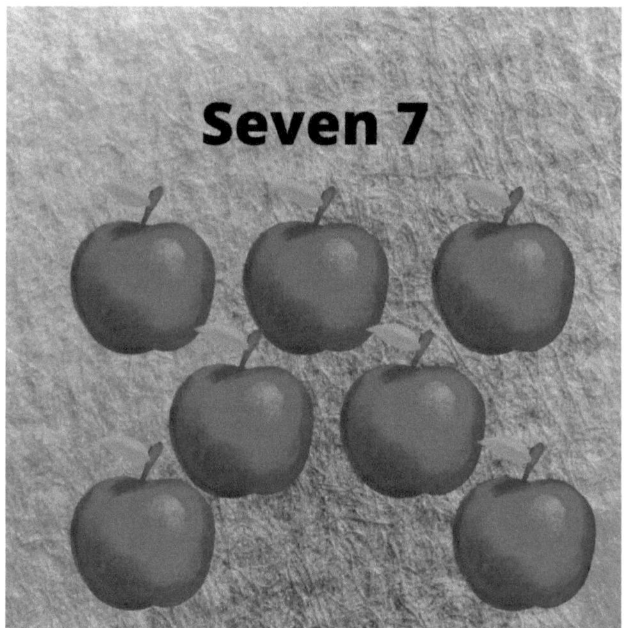

Seven apples

CHAPTER EIGHT

Number Eight

The boys went home. Thier mother reminded them of thier homework.The boys opened a pack of pencil which had eight pencils .They took the pencils and started writing.Thier mother was very happy and hugged them for being good boys.

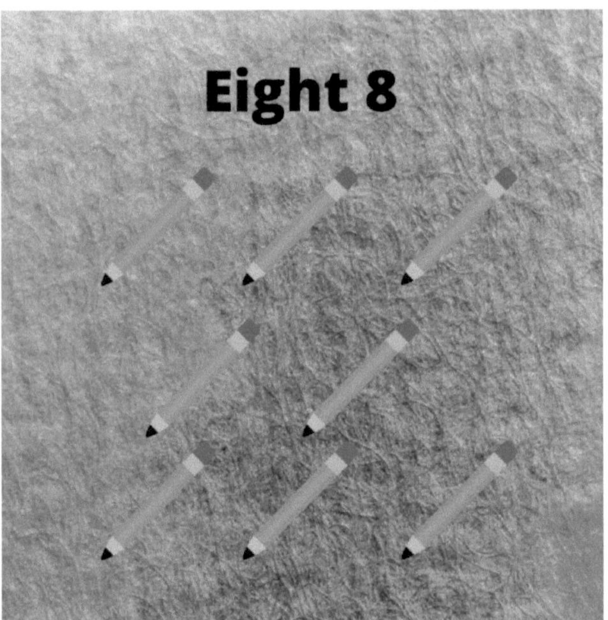

Eight pencils

CHAPTER NINE

Number Nine

Mother had got watermelon from the vegetable shop.She washed it and cut into nine pieces.Everyone at home enjoyed the juicy watermelon.

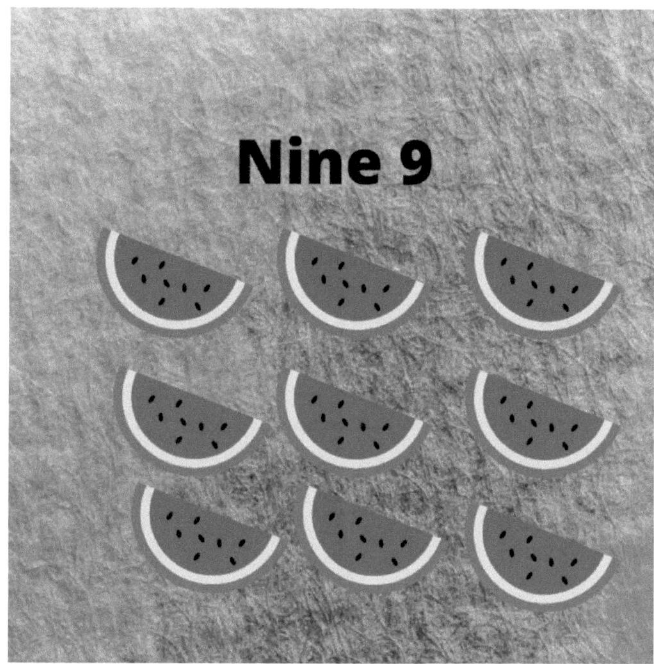

Nine watermelons

CHAPTER TEN

Number Ten

The kids had a wonderful day. They ate healthy watermelons and apples. They had finished thier homeworks as well.Thier granfather was happy to give the kids lollypops.He had ten lollypops which he distributed to the kids.

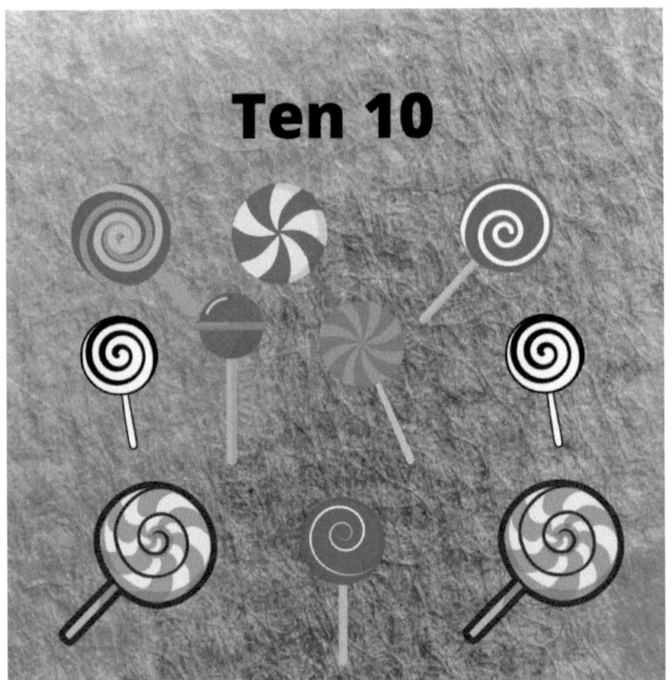

Ten lollypops

CHAPTER ELEVEN

Activity -1

Let us now refresh all that we learnt in our story.Throughout the story we learnt numbers from one to ten.Let us now count the number of objects of each type and tell it loud .

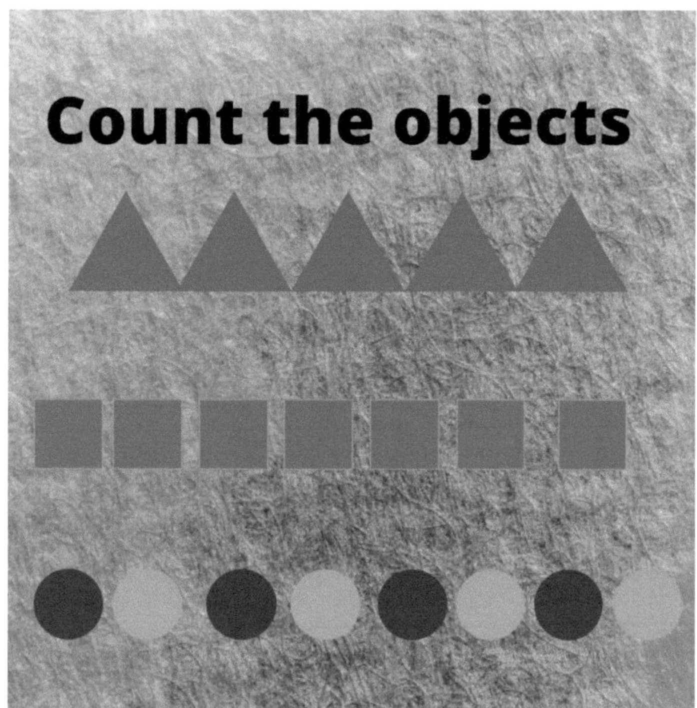

Count the objects

CHAPTER TWELVE

Activity - 2

Let us do some more counting .Keep up the learning spirit.

Count the similar objects

CHAPTER THIRTEEN

Activity - 3

Few more to go.Keep counting .

Count the similar objects in the above picture

CHAPTER FOURTEEN

Activity - 4

Last few numbers to go! Keep counting.

Count and tell it aloud

CHAPTER FIFTEEN

Activity - 5

Let us do some activity now. Count the number of objects and cirle the correct number you see on the right hand side.

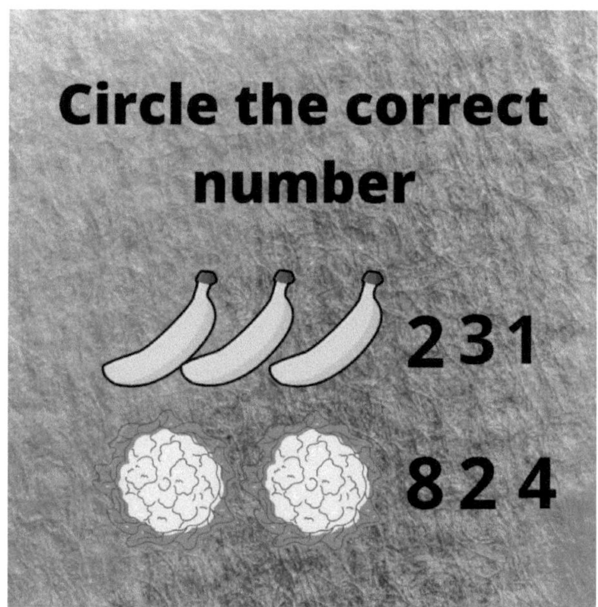

Count and circle

CHAPTER SIXTEEN

Activity - 6

Just one more to go . Cirlce the correct number of roses you see in the next picture.

Count and circle

9 798885 460316

Printed by Libri Plureos GmbH in Hamburg,
Germany